SOME APPROACHES TO A JUDGMENT IN PAINTING

SOME APPROACHES TO A JUDGMENT IN PAINTING

BY

SIR AUGUSTUS DANIEL

THE REDE LECTURE
1940

CAMBRIDGE
AT THE UNIVERSITY PRESS
1940

CAMBRIDGE
UNIVERSITY PRESS

University Printing House, Cambridge CB2 8BS, United Kingdom

Published in the United States of America by Cambridge University Press, New York

Cambridge University Press is part of the University of Cambridge.

It furthers the University's mission by disseminating knowledge in the pursuit of education, learning and research at the highest international levels of excellence.

www.cambridge.org
Information on this title: www.cambridge.org/9781107630956

First published 1940
Re-issued 2014

A catalogue record for this publication is available from the British Library

ISBN 978-1-107-63095-6 Paperback

SOME APPROACHES TO A JUDGMENT IN PAINTING

WHEN I was honoured with an invitation to give the Rede Lecture I need hardly say that I hesitated. I had rarely given a lecture. I had written no books and for many years I had but one almost constant interest and occupation, namely, that of examining pictures. On receiving the invitation I felt that on that subject and that subject alone I might have something to say.

I do not, however, propose to inflict upon you a list of my admirations; still less should I propose even to hint at the large number of works which leave me cold or with a feeling of distaste. These questions of approval and aversion, however crucial to the amateur seriously concerned with the arts, have always seemed to me essentially a private matter. But, it will be said, this cannot be true. Have we not been for the last century and more immersed in a stormy sea of conflict, each party asserting the absolute rightness of its judgment and the utter falseness of the other party's view of merit? Have we forgotten the indecent quarrels over the Pre-Raphaelite group of painters, the treatment of such poets as Keats, the reception of the *Lyrical Ballads*, the Wagner controversies?

Why should the field of art be so frequently a scene of bitter contests?

It may be said that man is a belligerent animal, who values little unless it be obtained by conquest. It is true also that in all important matters of daily practice there will be found those in possession and contented and those others who are envious and wish to gain at least their share. Even in intellectual matters, in science, in history, in theology, peace does not always prevail. But, I repeat, why should the field of art be invaded? Why should a matter of private enjoyment, the possession of which deprives no one of his equal share, be obscured and buried in the fumes of contest?

Let us grant that artists, having a message to deliver, should chafe at the density of their public who prefer the old and the customary. They are bound to advocate their view. But if I am right in believing that the enjoyment of fine things is a private affair, I feel justified in asking whether the lovers of art need join in these debates. Furthermore, I am convinced that the nature of art itself forbids. If a picture or poem is indifferent and awakens no echo in the mind, let it lie. If it is to you a true work of art, study and enjoy it.

I propose in this lecture to outline some of the doctrines which have given rise to conflict, and show what I believe to be their fallacies. I shall try also to give the reasons why the very nature of the fine arts should exclude partisanship. To put it briefly, if a picture or poem is truly fine, it is its own advocate. If the observer cannot refrain from demanding from the work what it does not contain, the fault lies with the observer and he should be silent. It is the wilful introduction of private views, abstract doctrines and personal preferences which creates the tumult and misleads the amateur.

I may be excused from entering the lists on one side or the other of the frequent conflicts in which artists and critics have been engaged during the last thirty years. I propose instead to take certain views held by distinguished writers in the past and warmly contested in their time, and I will quote first a few lines from *Modern Painters*.

John Ruskin, in the second chapter of the first volume, where he is laying down, once and for all as he believes, a definition of Greatness in Art, says: "Painting or Art generally as such with all its technicalities, difficulties and particular ends is nothing but a noble vehicle of thought, but by itself nothing."

This statement uttered by Ruskin with his accustomed passionate conviction would be as passionately denied by many to-day, if not in the past, and he himself denies its truth almost in the same breath. "It is not," he says, "however, easy either in painting or in literature to determine where the influence of language stops and where that of thought begins. Many thoughts are so dependent upon the language in which they are clothed that they would lose half their beauty if otherwise expressed." Still, not to be defeated by his unseen opponents, he continues: "But the highest thoughts are those which are least dependent on language, and the dignity of any composition and praise to which it is entitled are in exact proportion to its independency of language or expression."

It is easy to see how the youthful Ruskin came to announce this amazing doctrine. He strongly felt—and rightly felt—that the landscapes of Turner were finer than those of his contemporaries, and his zeal prompted him to attempt to prove their superiority. He had no difficulty in pointing to the far more varied and extensive use of natural fact and natural effects by Turner than his rivals or even his predecessors exhibited in their landscapes. Did it, therefore, follow that Turner landscapes are finer pictures than those of his rivals? To Ruskin, as to Wordsworth, Nature was a

Divine Creation. It was clear then to Ruskin that one who represented in his work the most and the best of Nature must be the greatest painter, if only his medium, the means by which Nature was represented, impeded as little as possible the passage from Nature to man as observer. To reduce this medium, the language of painting, if I may so call it, to a minimum seemed in thought an easy and even necessary step. This step John Ruskin boldly took.

I would ask you to note that Ruskin's proof of the superiority of Turner's landscape and his reduction of the language, the picture itself, to a negligible minimum, rests on the same logical process as that which occurs to the occasional and intermittent visitor to a gallery. The one asks: "What is that?" "It is Dutch boors in a cellar" or "It is The Madonna and Child", replies the other. The mind has leapt past the picture to a reality. A return may be made and the picture approved for its truthfulness to reality, but the picture has been used merely as a sign and has not been regarded in and for itself. It is little more than such perception of a door as is needed to turn the handle and enter the next room.

It is however clear that the individual work, whether picture or poem, is more than a sign, a bridge between reality and the observer. But before proceeding further with this point, I will mention another approach distinct from John Ruskin's and yet akin.

How frequently we find brilliant essays in which the writer, taking the works of an artist, draws from them as a whole certain characteristics of their maker! The assumption then is made that these characters are the full and clear expression of the artist's mind and personality. From this presumed character the writer, returning to this or that picture or poem, seeks in it, not what is there, but what of the author's character can be traced in his work. This method of approach is very frequent and perhaps inevitable. What should we do without the biographies of our great poets and artists?

A further assumption, largely fallacious also,

lies hidden in this approach; namely that the work of the artist is a pure product, without interference by chance, occasional mood or external influence. In truth, the character of the man is one thing, the character of the individual work is quite another thing. These two approaches, and others which I shall proceed to discuss, while concerned with works of art are, strictly speaking, using them for other purposes. John Ruskin was looking in the Turner landscapes for evidence of truth to Nature. The essayists are looking for evidence in the series of works of the poet or artist of certain general traits on which they may frame an image of the man. Neither look at the work in and for itself. Both pass beyond and talk of something else.

I will now turn to another approach, one most prevalent and always with us, and I will illustrate it from Sir Joshua Reynolds' famous *Discourses.*

Sir Joshua, as painter, could not waver in his conviction that the trained artist must choose what he paints and how he shall paint, and that, in fact, the work of art must be an arbitrary choice by the artist himself. But while admitting that the artist will and should paint as he wishes, Sir Joshua could not refrain, as scholar and amateur rather than as painter, from affirming that there is one manner of painting so superior that any others are almost negligible. He asserts that the art of painting gradually reached a summit in the works of Michelangelo and Raphael in the first half of the sixteenth century, and that the art has steadily deteriorated since that time. Individual painters, the Caracci, Rubens, Nicholas Poussin, are set apart, approved, and excused for not being of the higher manner; but the thesis is maintained.

In what is Sir Joshua's thesis an error? It is, I am convinced, an error from the point of view of the artist. If he has not an inborn inclination, it is little likely that he will bring to birth much of merit except perhaps in his earliest attempts. For the amateur, it is a false approach to come to a picture with mind prepared with a canon which demands that every work should be of a particular kind. The work of art is not an experiment according to a scientific law. Reynolds himself, with his accustomed candour, confesses that this view may be held to be on his part a prejudice. If the whole of the extant works of painting for the artist to study and the amateur to admire were confined solely to works of the Florentine and Roman schools before the middle of the sixteenth century, there would be little harm in his urgent advice. But there are other schools beside the Florentine and Roman, and other great masters beside Michelangelo and Raphael.

Furthermore, it is one thing to agree that the extant works of the old masters are the only objective standard. It is a very different thing to say that it is that style of painting which the artist should follow, if he can, and the amateur should exclusively seek and admire. Poets may be proud that there are the Homeric poems and the *Divine Comedy*, but very few would attempt to imitate them. Painters are proud that Michelangelo and Raphael have left behind them their masterpieces, but Rubens, Rembrandt, Titian and Velasquez have also left great works. The amateur cannot neglect the individual masterpieces of any one of these four, and it is in the singularity of each that he finds their beauty and his delight. All these, with many others, are food for his experience and a test for his eye; but to take them as grounds on which he may frame a rule which shall guide him in his judgment in future cases would be a serious error.

The heated discussions on the Grand Style have long passed away, and may or may not return. Nor is it the judgments of Sir Joshua and John Ruskin on individual works of painting on which I have been casting doubt, for both were distinguished amateurs with a wide experience of painting. So far from doubting I respect their judgments on individual pictures, and I fully understand their intensely felt preference for the works of certain painters. But to exalt their personal preference into a universal doctrine, and to advocate it with the eloquence and persuasiveness which both possessed, was harmful both to artist and amateur. For there are many who seek reasons for liking and disliking and who fear to approve and disapprove, and such authoritative utterances as these are bound to mislead. The born painter will force his way, despite doctrine, abuse, or neglect. But the mind of the amateur, who is without experience of practice in painting, is apt to be prejudiced by fallacies of this kind in his approach to new works, and his freedom of approach may be impeded over the whole field of art.

How then is the amateur to equip himself and defend himself from these dogmatic opinions? There are always with us dogmatic offenders of less open minds and of more intense personal preferences than even those two distinguished authors.

Let us admit that works of art are passive to every judgment, and that art and artists will always suffer painfully from the immediate judgment of the chance comer. Let us, therefore, put aside the judgment of the chance comer, and consider, as a supposition, the approach of the experienced amateur to an original work by an unknown painter; and by "original", I mean a work very different from those to which this observer has been accustomed. There are many pictures in our galleries which we can feel assured were at first received with astonishment by all, with ultimate approval by some, and with exasperation and denial by most of the contemporary amateurs.

Who might be expected to make the best approach to a right judgment of a new, an original work? I should suppose that he who had become lovingly attached to the best of the works of his own time might be willing to consider with care this new work. I feel sure that the amateur who had already established in his own mind a standard and special mode of painting, would in all probability summarily reject it. The work fails to present the character which he expected and does present characters which conflict with his standard.

How then may an amateur become experienced?

We must grant, I take it, that there is an initial liking for the art, whether it be for painting, poetry or music, and that this liking being present, the desire to see and hear such works is a constant and stable disposition of the mind. He may or may not also wish to add his own contribution to the multitude of such works in existence. In any case the desire will become a dominant interest.

As dominant interest, this desire will determine his movements, will select his friends, will direct his reading and will perhaps determine his life occupation. He should, I am convinced, constantly study the works of the old masters in the light of contemporary works, and contemporary works in the light of the old masters. However different in appearance, they are both products of the same art. The authority which the older masterpieces now possess is apt to check frank criticism; and, owing to the lack of authority, it is difficult out of the mass of contemporary work to distinguish the better from the indifferent. It is well, therefore, to remember that the much-prized masterpieces in our galleries are but those chosen from the mass of their contemporaries. Nor is the repute of some among the chosen at any date free from doubt. A temporary fashion may raise the reputation of this or that painter above his due height.

The amateur will gain much if he chance to have the privilege of meeting genuine artists, those, I mean, who with each work are setting themselves a new problem, one difficult to solve and requiring all their "originality". To examine paintings of other artists in company with one of these is an invaluable lesson. No one grasps the essence of a picture more quickly and more intensely than an artist of long practice and wide experience. He sees at once the main purpose, that aspect of the initial idea which particularly interested the painter and led him to proceed with it. He can distinguish the primary from the secondary aims and read it off as few amateurs can read it. If the picture is fine, he sees the relevance of every touch, every note of colour, every line and every passage of tone.

The amateur will also learn from artists how difficult their art is, and how rarely the execution or realization of the initial idea proceeds without a check. He will gather that the best part sometimes may be the result of chance. In a work which seems a success, not even the artist can tell how much of what he originally wished is still there, how much that he would have liked to retain has had to be sacrificed, and how much of what is there is there for lack of better.

This question of the creation or realization of a work of art, whether it be picture, poem or, I presume, symphony, has troubled many critics from olden days and it may be said that a discussion of it is foreign to the purpose of this lecture. That is true, or would be true if there were not so many wild and extravagant theories of the beautiful in art which are based upon the mysteries of its creation.

I propose, therefore, to add a little more, and I ask you to consider again Professor Housman's lecture on the Name and Nature of Poetry. It will be remembered that in this lecture Housman, half humorously, but also I believe, quite seriously, describes the process of the composition of a poem, as observed in himself. His description should be compared with a parallel description by the living French poet, M. Paul Valéry.[1] It is quite remarkable how alike the descriptions of the beginning, middle and end are in the two cases.

In [2]Housman's case two stanzas were given as he took a walk. A little later a third stanza emerged. The fourth and last stanza had to be made and the making took a twelvemonth. In Valéry's case a blank rhythmic figure of ten syllables possessed him and a desire to write a poem on this scheme followed. Under further consideration the blank decasyllabic verse became a figure of a certain number of stanzas, each of six verses, and the idea of a composition founded on this scheme of stanzas emerged.

[1] Paul Valéry. Variété III, "Au Sujet du 'Cimetière marin'", p. 68.

[2] A. E. Housman. "The Name and Nature of Poetry". Leslie Stephen Lecture, 1933, p. 50.

Valéry then relates that from this stage of realization the kind and nature of the final composition were conceived. Then, he adds, followed a long period of hard labour.

In these two parallel cases the initial idea appears as if by chance. Attention to this develops, not out of the blue but from the ground of the beginning, other elements of the as yet incomplete end. No mere attention seems able to obtain some members still lacking to the whole, and active attention and labour have to construct these; and thus the individual work comes into being.

The waywardness of the human mind is so great that it is most probable, if not certain, that no common rule of action in these matters could ever be obtained. But some consideration should be given to the problem by all who hope to put themselves in a position to judge the merits and demerits of works of art.

Early in the last century a discussion arose on the nature and distinction of Imagination and Fancy and incidentally on the character of the poet. It arose from Wordsworth's preface to the edition of his works published in 1815. Coleridge in his *Biographia Literaria* both criticized and, in part, approved of Wordsworth's views. As analysis of certain aspects of the individual poems themselves Wordsworth's distinctions are admirable, but transferred to the process of the creation of the work, they are much less appropriate. It is amusing as well as profitable to compare the views of Housman and Valéry with those of Wordsworth and Coleridge. With the former pair such terms as Imagination, Fancy and Genius are conspicuous by their absence. To the latter pair they are essential. For Wordsworth and Coleridge valid distinctions observed in the poems of Milton, Shakespeare and in Wordsworth's own work are transferred to their authors themselves, and in the minds of these are attributed to various almost independent faculties, which under the action of the individual will are made responsible for the character of the resulting work.

The difference between the two views may be said to lie in the distinctive psychological theories of their period. But it is doubtful whether the psychological grounds on which are based Wordsworth's and Coleridge's theories of creation would be held valid to-day, and it is certain that if they were so held to-day, they do not directly assist in the appreciation of the work of art. Like the other doubtful approaches to judgment in art, these also transcend the works themselves. The negative views of Housman and Valéry at least leave the field clear and summon the amateur to examine the works for themselves. Wordsworth and Coleridge are apt to raise a fog between the amateur and his object.

It would be foolish to attempt to condemn the use of such terms as Imagination and Fancy, and in their place they hold good. But as abbreviated expressions to describe the process of painting a picture or writing a poem they can be but partially true. To express the intense delight and complete satisfaction which the picture or poem gives by asserting that this work is a work of genius or of a vivid imagination is to say little or nothing.

In this outline of the course of training proper to the amateur, I shall be thought to have neglected some important branches of study. And it is true that there is an overwhelming number of histories of art, of histories of individual schools of painting and biographies of individual painters. To these may be added those researches on the Beautiful which form that part of Philosophy which is called Aesthetics. How far are these necessary or helpful to the amateur? To my mind, very little and indirectly only.

These studies are of course quite legitimate, and have been scrupulously pursued by many and very distinguished historians. But I am attempting to deal solely with the judgment of quality in works of art, and for the amateur it is extant pictures, frescoes and drawings which are his concern. His time must be mainly spent with these wherever they may be.

The historian will arrange extant works, and even non-existent works, in order of date of production, and that is so far to the good. But there is a danger in this approach. A

Giotto fresco may be for us as fine as any work produced later. Yet being taken as early, it may be held to be immature, as but a step to a better. It may even be silently assumed, on the ground of the general principle, that it is among the works of to-day that perfection is to be found. This, indeed, it would be difficult to admit. Again, without other encouragement the lover of the work of a particular artist will be irresistibly led to enquire how the painter struggled, lived, and fared. But after all the work itself is the prime record of the man, and records of the daily events of his life add little or nothing to the appreciation of the individual work.

It is perhaps closer to our purpose to arrange the works of a painter or poet in a series of the earlier and later, and to trace a sort of evolution or at least a change from the earlier to the later. But this approach again, though imposing on the student a minute and intensive analysis of each work, is yet as such irrelevant to our purpose. Each work of the series is singular and claims its own solution if a correct judgment is to be obtained. Along this by-path the amateur may be led to examine the early works of an artist with a view to trace the influences of predecessors and contemporaries; and they may be found. By very intelligent critics a picture or poem may be proved to be so little the work of one and so far the work of many that the nominal artist disappears in a mist.

Of Aesthetic—a complete theory, shall I say, of the Sublime and the Beautiful—I dare attempt no judgment. But I have a grave suspicion not only that the individual works of art disappear from view and with them their creators, but that what replaces them is but an empty rule without sanction for the artist and without authority for the amateur. In abstract sciences laws do exist somewhere and somehow and are guides in practice. With the work of art the worker equipped for his task makes and finds the rules for each work as it proceeds.

Now I do not deny that the amateur may gain much indirect aid from any or all of these approaches to art. There is no short cut to the desired end and, in fact, to the serious student some pursuit of the problems treated in the art histories, the biographies, even the theories of art is inescapable. And they may at times be most helpful. Some note or record may solve a puzzle in a work and remove an impediment to its full enjoyment. A picture seems dull and speechless; a word or the catalogue gives us the author's name and the work at once becomes eloquent. For other works by the artist have given us a key to his aims. Or again, a painting may appear under a great name. Willingly you would yield to it, but you cannot. It may well be your blindness. But sometimes a chance record or a hint from a student of his work appears and you are relieved. It is a copy. Yet I grudge the distraction which the reading of many books brings upon the amateur. I am grieved that the many masterpieces are not pursued and possessed as treasures in their own right.

There is one source of instruction for the amateur which was mentioned earlier in passing and deserves more consideration. That is the importance of the extant works of the recognized old masters. For Sir Joshua, living in the atmosphere of the Grand Style, they were all-important. It is true that he narrowed his choice too closely for opinion to-day, but he was ever ready to mark the excellence of those who stood next; a Titian, a Rubens, a Rembrandt. These masterpieces will certainly be to the experienced amateur a constant reminder of what the art of painting can do. He may also make them a severe test of his feeling and judgment. With patient and close attention he should examine them again and again. Their greatness is not on the surface. Their scale, their completion, their variety, their mastery of the whole art are almost paralysing. It is not easy to be frank with them as with much modern work. It is very easy to accept them on authority and, in fact, not feel the admiration which you declare. But full insight into a great Rubens or Rembrandt is a complete reward for years of labour in many galleries.

It may be said that professing to deal with

approaches to a judgment in painting, I have made much, even too much, use of the experience of poets and the nature of poetry. It may be added that while the use of language in poetry is inevitable, the use of the word "language" for painting is merely metaphorical.

For the painter, the expression on the canvas of his purpose is by stroke of brush or pencil, by the set of pigments on his palette, by the proper adjustment of the loaded brush to each element of the composition as it comes into being. There is a continuous invention of his parts of speech throughout the painting of each individual picture.

To the poet his language is, in a sense, supplied ready made. But the words he selects are of a special kind and for a special purpose. It is true that the same ready-made supply is also used for other purposes, in day-to-day practice, to describe, to converse, and to inform others what he knows, what he needs, what he proposes. But the poet in making a poem, I imagine, selects each word and phrase much as the painter adjusts each stroke of the brush, in the light of the composition which he has in mind. I would even venture to assert that the selection of the word is rather an invention of a use in this particular context than the use of it here in its casual meaning of day-to-day practice. May it not even be said that a word in a scrupulously wrought poem gains an unique character, proper to itself, and never to be attained elsewhere? The use of a word in a fine poem, its sound, colour, meaning, is bound up with and displayed in the poem as an individual unity. To pursue, however, this analysis further is beyond my powers, but the more closely the point is considered, the clearer will, I believe, the kinship of the two become. A further proof may be seen in the identical use or rather misuse of the "language" of both—in the case of painting, the painted canvas, in the case of poetry, the written or spoken poem. In both cases what is before one, whether seen or heard, may be treated as a mere sign and itself ignored. What the picture depicts and the poem describes may be taken, and wrongly taken, as their sole or primary purposes.

With some trepidation I propose now to enter into what is suspiciously like the dim regions of metaphysics and I am going to quote some passages from F. H. Bradley's *Appearance and Reality*. It would perhaps be tedious and take too long to quote in full, and I shall recklessly extract those passages which are relevant to my purpose. In the last chapter but one, entitled, "The Absolute and its Appearances", Mr Bradley writes: "In the aesthetic attitude we may seem to have transcended the opposition of idea to existence and to have at last surmounted and risen beyond the relational consciousness." That is, to cheapen the thought, we may seem momentarily to have gained an attitude in which the present existence seems perfect and both feeling and thought are satisfied, and contented to rest in the here and now, to maintain it and not to seek beyond. He continues: "For the aesthetic attitude seems to retain the immediacy of feeling. And it has also an object with a certain character, but yet an object self-existent and not merely ideal." Again to comment: that object is on the one hand the mere picture or poem, but on the other hand as present, perceived and felt it becomes, as Bradley states further on, the self-existent emotional and the self-existent pleasant and, therefore, he adds, actually pleasant to someone.

And it is in the last quality that the source of the many conflicting opinions lies. For this "someone" is all the many someones. And there are those who seek for truth to Nature as the ground of their approval or disapproval; there are others for whom the Michelangelesque is the basis, and yet others for whom it may be that criticism of life alone suffices.[1] There are also the many others for whom less worthy grounds are sufficient.

I apologise for inflicting upon my audience at this late moment these patches torn from a closely woven metaphysical texture. I well know that metaphysical aphorisms, isolated from their context, are as misleading in any subject as abstract theories are in matter of art.

[1] Cf. Matthew Arnold. Essays in Criticism, Series II. "The Study of Poetry."

But it was comforting to me after my long frequentation with art and its problems to gather from the side of metaphysics corroboration of the view to which I was gradually being driven by my own experience.

The work of appreciating a picture or poem is not an easy task. It takes time and requires close analysis and attention. Each individual work should be regarded as a problem. It is a problem not for thought but for feeling; not for mere feeling but for the feeling of those experienced in that art whether artist or amateur. It is only gradually that the object becomes distinguished and that it is possessed in all its details. Only after the distinguished object is thus possessed and felt as a series of concordant elements and felt with pleasure, delight or awe, only then is valid the judgment of its excellence. Once possessed and now seen again, it is as when one recognizes a friend as friend and no stranger. The object is at once recognized in all its richness, and for that observer it has become a living work of art.

What is so experienced by one may leave another quite untouched. Nor does the particular judgment remain always the same. The self, the experience, changes. It may become more severe or less interested. What once delighted may cease to delight.

At the beginning of this paper I said that approval and aversion were a private matter. I now venture to add that the momentary character of judgments in painting and other arts, their uncertainty and instability, are such that they are better kept private so that freedom of judgment may be preserved.

I may perhaps summarize the conclusions of my lecture in a few dogmatic statements.

(1) There are no criteria or principles for judging whether a picture or poem is in truth a fine work of art.

(2) It is only the experienced amateur—be he artist or poet or neither—who will feel the subtleties, the intimate relationship of element to element, of part to part, throughout their union.

(3) For a true work of art is an individual

whole and both the unity and its diversity have to be felt and understood each in all and all in each.

(4) Doubtless the archaeologist, the grammarian, the historian or the biographer may use a work of art and quite legitimately find what he seeks. But he is treating the object not as an aesthetic object but as one containing some evidence, some record or some feature of interest, in his particular subject. This feature he abstracts from the individual whole, and uses it, ignoring the rest.

For EU product safety concerns, contact us at Calle de José Abascal, 56–1°, 28003 Madrid, Spain or eugpsr@cambridge.org.

www.ingramcontent.com/pod-product-compliance
Ingram Content Group UK Ltd.
Pitfield, Milton Keynes, MK11 3LW, UK
UKHW040723120726
473066UK00028B/248

* 9 7 8 1 1 0 7 6 3 0 9 5 6 *